Eat Your Vegetables! Drink Your Milk!

Dr. Alvin Silverstein,

Virginia Silverstein, and

Laura Silverstein Nunn

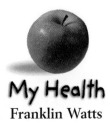

My Health

Franklin Watts

A Division of Grolier Publishing

New York • London • Hong Kong • Sydney

Danbury, Connecticut

Photographs©: Envision: 4 (Peter Johansky), 32, 36 (George Mattei), 7, 8, 10, 38 (Steven Needham); Monkmeyer Press: 29 (Patrick Clark); Photo Researchers: 16 (Margot Granitsas), 6 (Phillip Hayson), 23 (Chris Marona), 39 (Astrid & Hanns Frieder Michler/SPL), 17, 19, 22 (Charles D. Winters); PhotoEdit: 35 (Mary Kate Denny), 31 bottom (Myrleen Ferguson), 12 (Robert Ginn), 34 (Spencer Grant), 15 (Felicia Martinez), 30, 33 (Michael Newman), 14, 31 top (David Young-Wolff); Tony Stone Images: 9 (Thomas Del Brase).

Cartoons by Rick Stromoski; medical illustration on page 27 by Leonard Morgan

Visit Franklin Watts on the Internet at:
http://publishing.grolier.com

Library of Congress Cataloging-in-Publication Data

Silverstein, Alvin.
 Eat your vegetables! Drink your milk! / by Alvin Silverstein, Virginia Silverstein, and Laura Silverstein Nunn.
  p.   cm.—(My Health)
 Includes bibliographical references and index.
 Summary: Describes the components of a healthful diet and explains why eating these foods is important for maintaining overall good health.
  ISBN 0-531-16507-8 (lib. bdg.)   0-531-16507-8 (pbk.)
  1. Nutrition—Juvenile literature. [1. Nutrition.] I. Silverstein, Virginia B. II. Nunn, Laura Silverstein. III. Title. IV. Series.
 QP141.S5326 2000
 613.2—dc21   99-049740
                                               CIP

Contents

Food for Life

What is your favorite food? Do you like chocolate milkshakes, french fries, and pizza? Maybe you'd rather have a juicy peach or ripe cherries. You eat these foods because they taste good, but you also eat them to grow big and strong and to stay healthy.

The foods you eat give you the energy you need to run, play games, and do your schoolwork. If you don't eat a variety of healthful foods, you may feel tired and weak. You may even get cranky or have problems thinking clearly. That's why your parents say things like "Eat your vegetables!" and "Drink your milk!"

Did You Know...

The average adult in the United States eats more than 1,000 pounds (454 kilograms) of food each year.

◀ **Is pizza your favorite food?**

"Milk Does a Body Good"

Is it true what those milk ads say? You can't always believe what you see on TV, but milk really is the most nutritious of all foods. A newborn baby's first food is milk. Milk helps a baby to grow and develop. Studies show that children who drink milk grow faster than children who eat a good diet, but do not drink milk.

Some people don't like milk though. That's okay. Other foods have calcium too. You can drink orange juice with calcium added or eat plenty of green leafy vegetables to get the calcium you need.

Milk helps you grow.

What kinds of food do you eat? A balanced diet includes a variety of foods with the **nutrients** your body needs to work well. When you eat the right foods in the right amounts, you will be the best that you can be.

A balanced diet includes a variety of foods that provide the nutrients the body needs.

You Are What You Eat

You have a lot of choices when it comes to what to eat. Should you have cereal and milk with fruit for breakfast? Maybe bacon and eggs with toast would be better? For lunch, should you choose a tuna fish sandwich or peanut butter and jelly? Should your after-school snack be an apple or a bag of pretzels? For dinner, should you eat steak and potatoes, chicken with rice, or macaroni and cheese? It can be tough to make healthy food choices, but a **food guide pyramid** can help.

A food guide pyramid shows you the kinds and amounts of food you need every day. The foods in the

The food guide pyramid shows the kinds and amounts of food you need each day.

pyramid are grouped according to the nutrients they provide. For example, milk, yogurt, and cheese are rich in calcium, vitamin D, and protein.

You should eat a lot of the foods shown at the bottom of the pyramid. These include bread, cereal, rice, and pasta. You need a lot of fruits and vegetables too. Milk, yogurt, cheese, meat, poultry, fish, dry beans, eggs, and nuts are higher up on the pyramid. These are good foods, but you should not eat too much of them.

Fruits and vegetables contain plenty of good nutrients.

Fats, oils, and sweets are at the top of the pyramid. You don't really need these foods to stay healthy, but they can help make other foods taste better. For instance, you may like bread better with butter on it, or you may sprinkle sugar on your cereal.

You may also like to eat sweet foods by themselves, but you should think of gum, candies, and chocolate bars as special treats. It's okay to eat these foods once in a while, but you shouldn't eat them instead of other foods on the pyramid. Sweets will give you energy and some nutrients, but eating too many sweets can make you fat.

Candy, cakes, and other sweet snacks should make up only a small part of your diet.

Activity 1:
What's on TV?

What you see on TV can affect what you eat. The next time you sit down to watch a TV program, pay attention to what the characters are eating. Can you see the brand names of the foods? Make a list of all the foods you can identify.

Pay attention to the commercials too. Every time you see a commercial for a food item, write down what is being advertised and describe the commercial.

When the program is over, look at the food pyramid in this book and think about the following questions:

- Were the characters in the show eating healthful foods?
- Would you like to try a new food because a character you like was eating it?
- How many of the commercials advertised foods in the bread and cereal group?
- How many commercials tries to sell foods in each of the other groups?
- Do TV ads show some food groups more than others?

A sausage pizza fits into several food groups.

Where would you put a sausage pizza on the food pyramid? Actually, it fits into several different groups. The sausage is from the group that includes meat, poultry, fish, dry beans, eggs, and nuts. The cheese is in the dairy group. The tomato sauce is part of the vegetable group. The crust of the pizza belongs in the bread, cereal, rice, and pasta group.

Many of the foods you eat fit into more than one food group. Tuna casserole, a blueberry muffin, and a peanut butter and jelly sandwich are some examples. Can you think of some others?

Food Around the World

What you eat may depend on where you live. People who live in Mexico eat a lot of corn and corn products. People who live in Asian countries, such as China and Japan, eat rice every day. People who live near the ocean eat fish and seafood. In Italy, pasta is a popular dish. In the United States, people eat a wide variety of foods because foods are shipped in from all over the world.

What's in Your Food?

What do you think about when you take a bite out of a juicy peach or a crunchy apple? These foods taste good, and they are also good for you. They contain nutrients that your body needs. As your body digests, or breaks down, the foods, the nutrients are released.

A crunchy apple tastes good and is good for you too.

Important nutrients include **carbohydrates, proteins, fats, vitamins, minerals,** and water. Each kind of nutrient works differently in your body.

Carbohydrates are your body's main source of energy. There are two types of carbohydrates—starches and sugars. Starchy foods, such as bread, pasta, potatoes, and rice, usually contain many other important nutrients. Sugary foods, such as soda and candy, have very few other nutrients. Carbohydrates are broken down inside the body into a simple sugar called *glucose*. Glucose is the fuel used by the cells in your body.

Bread, pasta, potatoes, and grains contain plenty of carbohydrates, along with other important nutrients. Legumes like peas and beans are good sources of protein too.

Meat, fish, poultry, eggs, cheese, and milk are all good sources of protein.

Proteins give you energy, but they do other important things too. The proteins in meat, cheese, and eggs help to build bones, hair, muscles, and skin. While you are growing, you need a lot of protein. Adults need proteins too. They help replace worn-out body parts. The proteins in foods also contain materials that help control the body's activities.

Proteins are made up of smaller building blocks called **amino acids**. Our bodies have to break the proteins we eat into amino acids before they can be used to build the kinds of proteins we need.

Fats are found in butter, cheese, margarine, oil, and meat. Too much fat is not good for you, but you do need some. You can get all the fats you need from foods shown on other parts of the pyramid. Like carbohydrates, fats are broken down and used for energy. They are also used to protect your body organs, keep you warm, and build nerves that carry messages from one part of your body to another.

Surprises in Your Food

Foods contain many natural chemicals, but the companies that make foods sometimes add other chemicals. They want to make foods look better, taste better, or stay fresh longer. These chemicals are called **food additives**. Some companies add vitamins and minerals to help you stay healthy. For example, calcium is added to some kinds of orange juice, iodine is added to salt, and niacin is added to some breads.

All these foods contain fats. You need some fat in your diet, but not too much.

Activity 2: Testing for Fats

How can you tell which foods contain a lot of fat? Test some different kinds of foods. You might want to try butter, hamburger, french fries or potato chips, carrots, milk, and apple juice.

Cut several 3-inch (7-cm) squares out of a brown paper bag and label each square with the name of one of the foods you are testing. If the food is a solid, rub some of it onto the square. If the food is a liquid, put a few drops of it on the square. Let the squares dry and then hold each square up to a light. If light shines through the square, the food contains a lot of fat.

Your body also needs tiny amounts of vitamins and minerals every day. Vitamins help turn other nutrients into energy. They also help build bones, body tissues, and blood cells. Some vitamins help protect you from diseases.

Vitamin Pills

If you eat a healthy diet, you probably get all the vitamins and minerals you need. But sometimes it's hard to eat just the right variety of foods. People who think they may not be getting enough nutrients from food often take vitamin pills called **supplements**. Your body can't tell the difference between vitamin supplements and the natural nutrients it gets from foods.

Be careful, though. Too much of certain vitamins or minerals can be harmful. The daily vitamin supplements sold at most drugstores are safe. Some people think of them as nutritional insurance.

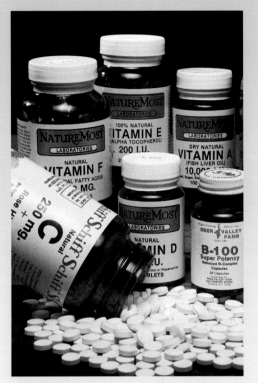

Some people take vitamin pills to get extra nutrients.

Like vitamins, minerals help build bones, blood cells, and teeth. Some important minerals are calcium, phosphorus, and iron. Nearly everyone loves the taste of salt, which contains the minerals sodium and chloride. You could not live without these minerals, but too much salt can cause high blood pressure in some people.

Some Important Vitamins and Minerals

Nutrient	What It Does	Food Sources
Vitamin A	Keeps eyes, skin, and hair healthy. Helps form teeth and bones. Helps keep body's defenses strong.	Broccoli, carrot, cantaloupe, **dairy products**, eggs, spinach, sweet potatoes
B vitamins (B1, B2, B3, B6, B12)	Help the body use nutrients. Help keep brain and nerves healthy. Help to heal injuries and fight disease. Help keep skin and eyes healthy.	Whole-grain breads, cereals, beans, peas, brown rice, nuts
Vitamin C	Helps to hold body cells together, heal cuts, and fight disease. Helps keep gums healthy. Helps in forming teeth and bones.	Broccoli, cantaloupe, cauliflower, lemons, oranges, limes, grapefruits, kiwis, tomatoes, potatoes
Vitamin D	Helps to build strong bones and teeth. Helps to keep the right amounts of calcium and phosphorus in the blood.	Butter, eggs, margarine, milk
Vitamin E	Helps to make muscles and red blood cells. Helps to protect body tissues from damage.	Eggs, fish, leafy vegetables, dry beans, nuts, peanuts, peas, whole-grain breads and cereals.
Vitamin K	Helps to stop bleeding. Helps keep bones strong and healthy.	Cabbage, cauliflower, cereals, dairy products, eggs, green leafy vegetables, meats, peas, tea

Nutrient	What It Does	Food Sources
Calcium	Helps to build bones and teeth. Helps muscles to contract. Helps nerves to send messages. Helps to stop bleeding.	Dairy products, dark green vegetables, dry beans, grapefruits, lemons, limes, oranges, peas, salmon, sardines, shellfish, tofu
Chloride	Helps to digest food. Helps to keep body fluids in balance.	Salt and most foods
Iron	Helps blood carry oxygen to body cells.	Dark leafy vegetables, eggs, dry beans, liver, meat, nuts, seeds, peas, whole-grain and enriched bread and cereals
Phosphorus	Helps to build bones and teeth. Helps body get energy from food. Helps muscles and nerves work well.	Dairy foods, eggs, fish, legumes, meat, nuts, poultry, whole-grain breads
Sodium	Helps to keep body fluids in balance. Needed for healthy muscles and nerves.	Salt and most foods

Water is one of the most important nutrients in your body. It makes up 50 to 70 percent of your weight and is needed for many of the chemical reactions that take place inside you. You drink only about half of the water you need. The rest comes from the foods you eat, such as fruits and vegetables.

What Is Fiber?

Fiber is the tough part of vegetables, grains, and fruits. It is not a nutrient, but it is an important part of a balanced diet. Fiber helps to carry away the body's solid wastes. Foods with a lot of fiber—such as beans, cabbage, broccoli, and onions—often cause gas. The gas is produced by bacteria that feed on the fiber.

Fruits, vegetables, and whole grains provide the fiber you need.

Breaking Down Food

Picture some of your favorite foods—a peanut butter and jelly sandwich, a slice of pizza, a banana split sundae, or a beefy taco. Does your mouth water as you think about these tasty foods? Your body is preparing for the long series of processes it uses to digest food.

Does this banana split sundae make your mouth water?

During digestion, foods go through some big changes. Even the tiniest crumbs are too big to fit into your body's cells, and the chemicals they contain are too complicated for a cell to handle. Most foods must be broken down into simpler substances before your body can use them.

Digestion starts the moment food enters your mouth. **Salivary glands** in your mouth pour out watery *saliva* to moisten the food and begin the break down of starches. As you chew, your teeth cut up the food and grind it into smaller pieces. These

Digestion starts in your mouth. As you chew an apple, it mixes with saliva produced by salivary glands.

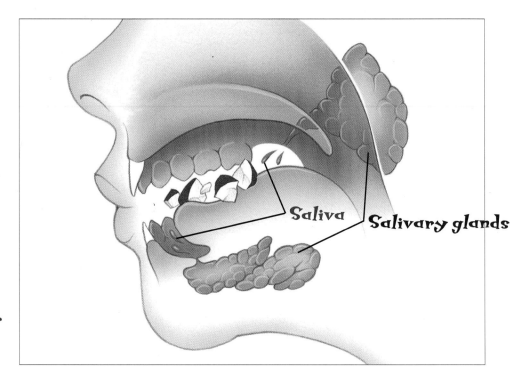

Saliva   Salivary glands

pieces are slowly broken down as the food travels through a long passageway inside your body called the **digestive tract.** The digestive tract begins at the mouth and ends at the *anus*, an opening where unused materials leave the body.

After you swallow food, it moves down your *esophagus*, a tube that leads to your stomach. There the food mixes digestive juices. Then it passes into a long, thin, coiled tube called the **small intestine**. The **pancreas** and the *liver* release more digestive juices into the small intestine. By this time, most of the

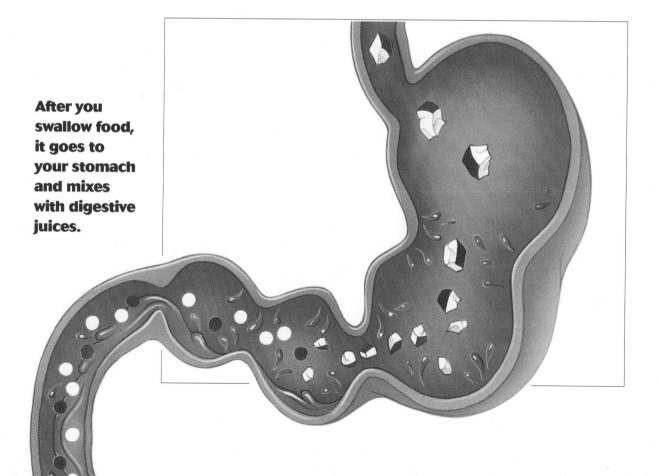

After you swallow food, it goes to your stomach and mixes with digestive juices.

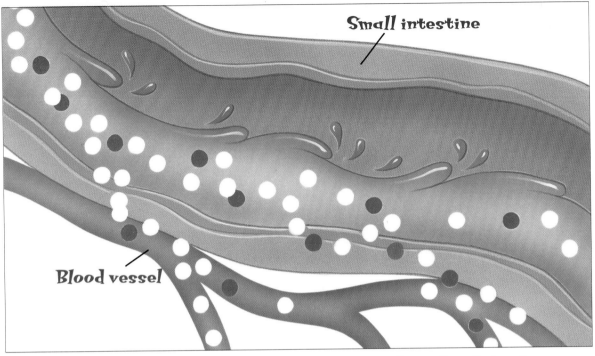

Small intestine

Blood vessel

By the time food reaches the small intestine, it has been broken down into particles small enough to pass into your blood vessels.

food has turned into a liquid mixture. Nutrients travel through the walls of the small intestine and enter your **blood vessels**. As blood flows through your body, it delivers nutrients to all your cells.

Some of the foods you eat cannot be digested. They continue to travel through your digestive tract. When they reach the end of the small intestine, they pass into a short, but wide, coiled tube called the **large intestine**. Extra liquid is absorbed into the blood, and the undigested food material leaves your body as **feces**. Most foods are digested in 4 to 8 hours, but some take as long as 24 hours to pass through the digestive tract.

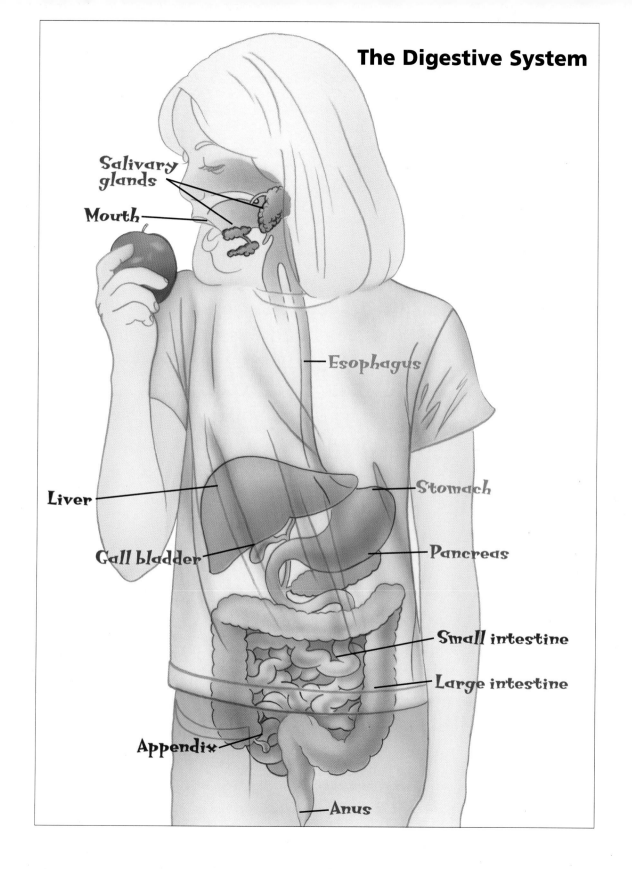

The Digestive System

Salivary glands

Mouth

Esophagus

Liver

Stomach

Gall bladder

Pancreas

Small intestine

Large intestine

Appendix

Anus

Eating the Right Amount of Food

Every day, thousands of chemical reactions take place inside your body. These chemical reactions build and repair the cells in your blood, muscles, nerves, and other body tissues. They also break down nutrients to provide energy. Scientists use the word **metabolism** to describe all the chemical reactions and body processes involved in nourishing your cells.

The processes going on inside your body use energy that comes from carbohydrates, proteins, and fats. The energy stored in these foods is measured in units called **calories**. One gram of protein or carbohydrate contains about 4 calories of energy. One gram of fat contains about 9 calories.

How many calories do you need every day? That depends

Did You Know...

A chocolate bar has 270 calories. To burn off the calories from one chocolate bar, you need to run for 14 minutes, walk for 52 minutes, or swim for 24 minutes.

Playing soccer, or other sports, uses up a lot of energy. You get the energy you need to stay active from the foods you eat.

on how old you are, how large your body is, and whether you are a boy or a girl. It also depends on how active you are. Do you play a lot of sports or do you spend a lot of time sitting at a desk studying? The more active you are, the more energy you use and the more calories you need. The average child needs about 2,300 calories a day to be healthy.

Can you eat just one potato chip? Junk foods taste good, but you should not eat too much of them.

Do you like to eat junk food—potato chips, soda, ice cream, cake, candy bars, and cookies? Junk food tastes good, but you shouldn't eat it too often. Most junk food has a lot of fat and calories. These foods give you quick energy, but they do not contain many nutrients.

Fats should make up about 30 percent of your diet. When you eat too much fat, your body will not burn all the calories. The extra calories are stored in fat cells found in certain parts of your body—especially your waist, thighs, and buttocks. As the extra calories build up, you gain weight.

People gain weight when they eat more food than their bodies need. Too much of any food can cause a weight problem. People who are seriously overweight are called **obese**. Millions of children in the United States are obese.

Carrying around a lot of extra fat puts a strain on the body. As a result, obese people often feel tired. They are also more likely than other people to develop serious health problems, such as cancer, diabetes, and heart disease.

How do you get rid of extra pounds? The best way to lose weight is to eat a balanced diet and cut down on the total amount of food you eat. You don't have to stop eating the foods you like. Just eat less of them. At the same time, you should exercise more. The more active you are, the more calories you'll burn. Remember, losing weight should be a gradual process.

Many people try to lose weight by **dieting**. There are many different kinds of diets. Some dieters think they

The best ways to lose weight are to eat smaller portions of a balanced diet (top) and to burn calories by exercising (bottom).

31

have to starve themselves to lose weight, but they are wrong. Not eating enough food can be very dangerous to your health. People who do not eat enough food or who eat the wrong kinds of foods may suffer from **malnutrition**.

People with malnutrition do not get all the nutrients their bodies need. They may become thin or weak. They may even get sick. A person should never go on a diet without talking with a doctor first. A doctor can help a person design a safe, healthy way to eat and lose weight.

When You Can't Eat Certain Foods

Do you get a rash when you eat strawberries? Do your eyes swell when you eat peanuts? If you get a bad reaction after eating a certain kind of food, then you probably have a food **allergy**. Common foods that can cause allergies include nuts, fish and shellfish, milk, eggs, pork, strawberries, oranges, and bananas. People with food allergies must find other foods that give them the nutrients they need.

Most people have no trouble eating peanuts, seafood, milk, strawberries, and eggs, but these foods can give some people an allergic reaction.

A healthy breakfast provides a good start to the day.

Which is your biggest meal? Breakfast? Lunch? Dinner? In the United States, many people skip breakfast. Then they have a small lunch and a big dinner. This is not a healthy way to eat.

Breakfast is the most important meal of the day. A good, healthy breakfast gives you the nutrients you need to walk, play—and think. Children who eat a healthy breakfast do better at school than those who skip breakfast.

These days, most people have very busy lives. Sometimes people are so busy that they forget to eat, or they grab a quick snack on the run. When they finally get home, they eat a large dinner. Actually, that is the worst time to eat a big meal. During the day, people are active and burn a lot of calories. Most people are less active at night.

What do you usually do after dinner? Sit down and watch TV? Read a book? Do your homework? These activities don't burn up many calories. Then, a few hours after eating, you go to bed. When you sleep, your metabolism slows down, so you burn very few calories while you sleep.

To maintain a healthy weight, it might make more sense to eat small meals spread throughout the day. Meals should consist of small, but satisfying portions. Between meals, have a healthy snack, such as fruit.

You use up very little energy while you are sleeping.

Healthy Eating

When you go shopping with your mom or dad, do you put some of your favorite foods in the cart? What kind of foods are they? You'd probably love to put in some potato chips, soda, cookies, or cupcakes. But as you know, these are not the best foods to eat. You need foods that contain a variety of nutrients.

Fresh fruit and vegetables are healthy choices when you are shopping for food.

You can find out exactly which nutrients a food contains by looking at the label. Reading food labels tells you the size of a serving and how many calories it contains. The label also lists the amount of fat, protein, carbohydrates, and various vitamins and minerals in the food. Food labels can help you make sure you are eating a balanced diet.

Food labels tell you what nutrients food products provide.

Activity 3:
Do You Eat a Balanced Diet?

Write down everything you eat for 1 week. At the end of the week, use what you've learned about nutrition to decide whether you eat a healthful diet. Do you eat too much junk food? Should you eat more vegetables? Do you skip meals? When it comes to food, what are your bad habits?

Most packaged foods also contain a list of ingredients. These are useful for people who are allergic to certain foods or those with medical conditions that limit what they can eat. For example, some people have to avoid eating too much salt or certain kinds of amino acids.

Can people who don't eat meat stay healthy? These people, called **vegetarians**, can eat a balanced diet and be healthy. But they have to

CONTAINS:
SALT
FAT
SUGAR
CAFFIENE

NEW
SNAX

choose foods carefully to make sure they get enough protein. Some vegetarians eat dairy products and eggs. These foods contain proteins. Other vegetarians eat only foods that come from plants. They must mix foods, such as beans and rice, to get all the protein they need. If you are a vegetarian, you should let a doctor help you create a balanced diet.

A vegetarian diet can be healthy and good tasting, but it must be carefully balanced.

When in Doubt, Throw it Out!

What's that green fuzzy stuff growing on that peach? It's mold. Molds grow on foods when they sit around too long. Mold tells you that the food is not safe to eat.

Many foods need to be refrigerated, or they will go bad quickly. Leftovers should never be left out at room temperature. The kinds of bacteria that can make you sick grow very quickly in warm temperatures.

You can't always tell if food is safe just by looking at it. If a food looks funny or smells strange, it's probably not good to eat. But don't taste it to see if it's bad—it could make you sick. Just remember: When in doubt, throw it out!

Yuck! These moldy foods have sprouted fungal growths. Spoiled foods may taste bad and can make you sick.

Healthy eating is the key to healthy living. Here are some good reasons to eat a balanced diet:
- You will have more energy.
- You will have healthy bones, teeth, skin, and hair.
- You will do better in sports and get better grades in school.
- You can fight off illnesses and avoid serious diseases.
- You can feel good about yourself.

Glossary

allergy—an unpleasant reaction to certain substances

amino acid—a building block from which proteins are made

anus—the opening from which wastes leave the body

blood vessel—one of the tubes that carries blood through the body

calorie—a measurement of the amount of energy that food gives you

carbohydrate—a starch or sugar, a nutrient that provides the body with energy

dairy product—milk or foods made from milk, such as cheese, yogurt, and ice cream

dieting—eating less food, or less of certain kinds of food, to lose weight

digestive tract—the tubelike passage inside the body in which food is digested. It extends from the mouth to the anus and includes the esophagus, stomach, and intestines

esophagus—the tube that carries food from the mouth to the stomach

fat—a high-energy nutrient, the main energy storage area in the body

feces—the body's solid wastes

fiber—the part of a plant that a person cannot digest

food additive—a chemical added to food to improve its taste, to make it look better, or to increase its nutritional value

food guide pyramid—a diagram showing the kinds and amounts of foods that make up a balanced diet

glucose—a simple sugar used as fuel by body cells

large intestine—the coiled tubelike part of the digestive tract between the small intestine and the anus. It absorbs excess water and prepares food that cannot be digested for leaving the body.

liver—a large organ that produces a liquid called bile, which helps digest food

malnutrition—a condition that results from not eating enough food or eating the wrong kinds of foods

metabolism—all the chemical reactions that go on in the body

mineral—a chemical in foods that is used to build blood cells, bones, and teeth. Calcium, phosporus, and iron are minerals.

nutrient—a chemical in food that is used by the body

obese—seriously overweight

pancreas—an organ that produces digestive juices

protein—a nutrient made up of amino acids. Proteins provide energy and help build and repair bones, hair, muscles, and skin.

saliva—a watery fluid in your mouth that helps you swallow and digest food

salivary gland—one of the organs that produces saliva

small intestine—the coiled tubelike part of the digestive tract between the stomach and the large intestine. It breaks down food so that nutrients can be absorbed into blood vessels.

supplement—a substance taken in addition to food to provide extra nutrients

vegetarian—a person who eats only foods from plants (fruits, vegetables, and grains), or foods from plant sources plus dairy products and/or eggs

vitamin—an essential nutrient found in small amounts in foods. Vitamins work in various chemical reactions to keep the body healthy.

Learning More

Books

Bennett, Paul. *Healthy Eating*. Parsippany, NJ: Silver Press, 1997.

Figtree, Dale. *Eat Smart*: *A Guide to Good Health for Kids*. Clinton, NJ: New Win Publishing, Inc., 1992.

Galperin, Anne. *Nutrition*. New York: Chelsea House Publishers, 1991.

Kalbacken, Joan. *The Food Pyramid*. Danbury, CT: Children's Press, 1998.

_____. *Food Safety*. Danbury, CT: Children's Press, 1998.

_____. *Vitamins and Minerals*. Danbury, CT: Children's Press, 1998.

McGinty, Alice B. *Eating Right*. New York: The Rosen Publishing Group, Inc., 1997.

Stille, Darlene R. *The Digestive System*. Danbury, CT: Children's Press, 1997.

Organizations and Online Sites

American Cancer Society
1599 Clifton Road NE
Atlanta, GA 30329-4251

The American Dietetic Association
216 West Jackson Blvd., Suite 800
Chicago, IL 60606-6995

Child/Adolescent Nutrition & Health
http://ificinfo.health.org/index3.htm
This site was developed and is maintained by the International Food Information Council Foundation. It has information about nutrition for children and teens, online brochures about healthy eating, and reports on special nutrition topics.

Children's Health and Nutrition
http://ericps.ed.uiuc.edu/npin/respar/texts/health.html
This site includes information on childhood obesity, the importance of eating breakfast, and the benefits of vitamin C.

Count Your Calories Because Calories Count!
http://www.bgsm.edu/nutrition/in.html
This site features online nutrition quizzes and a calorie calculator.

FDA/CFSAN For Kids and Educators
http://vm.cfsan.fda.gov/~dms/educate.html
This Food and Drug Administration site includes a food-safety coloring book, online quizzes, and even a song, "Germs on the Run."

Food and Drug Administration
Office of Consumer Affairs
5600 Fishers Lane, HFE-88
Rockville, MD 20857

The Food Guide Pyramid—For You
http://ificinfo.health.org/brochure/pyramid.htm
This site was developed and is maintained by the International
Food Information Council Foundation. It explains how to use
the food guide pyramid to develop a balanced diet.

Food and Nutrition Information Center
Agricultural Research Service, USDA
National Agricultural Library, Room 304
10302 Baltimore Avenue
Beltsville, MD 20705-2351

Healthy Eating at Foodwatch
http://www.foodwatch.com.au/
The site includes food quizzes and activities with such titles as
"Rate Your Weight," "Label Lingo," "10 Tips to Tame Fussy
Eaters," and "Recipes for Health."

Index

About the Authors

Dr. Alvin Silverstein is a Professor of Biology at the College of Staten Island of the City University of New York. **Virginia Silverstein** is a translator of Russian scientific literature. The Silversteins first worked together on a research project at the University of Pennsylvania. Since then, they have produced 6 children and more than 150 published books for young people.

Laura Silverstein Nunn, a graduate of Kean College, has been helping with her parents' books since her high school days. She is the coauthor of more than twenty books on diseases and health, science concepts, endangered species, and pets. Laura lives with her husband Matt and their young son Cory in a rural New Jersey town not far from her childhood home.